Creepy, Crawly Caterpillars

by Margery Facklam

Illustrated by Paul Facklam

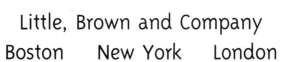

Little, Brown and Company

Boston　New York　London

Also by Margery Facklam and Paul Facklam
The Big Bug Book

To Mom and Dad—P. F.

First Edition

Library of Congress Cataloging-in-Publication Data

Facklam, Margery.
    Creepy, crawly caterpillars / by Margery Facklam : illustrated by
Paul Facklam. — 1st ed.
        p.   cm.
    ISBN 0-316-27342-2
    1. Caterpillars—Juvenile literature.   [1. Caterpillars.]
I. Facklam, Paul, ill. II. Title.
QL544.2.F33   1996
595.78′043—dc20   93-41443

10 9 8 7 6 5 4 3 2
First Printing
SC

Printed in Hong Kong

Contents

From Crawling to Flying in Four Easy Steps

Creepy, crawly *caterpillars* are everywhere—except the North and South Poles and on icy mountaintops. There are thousands of different kinds, and not one looks like its parents. Caterpillars may appear to be worms, but they are insects. A worm is always a worm, but a caterpillar is only a caterpillar for a little while before it changes into a butterfly or moth.

Some caterpillars are so small that they can live inside a flat leaf. Others are as big as a fat cigar. But all caterpillars have the same basic equipment. Their bodies are divided into thirteen segments. The first segment is the head, with twelve tiny eyes called *ocelli.* A caterpillar doesn't see much more than light and dark, and the shadowy figure of anything that moves. It doesn't have much of a brain, but it gets information about where it is with a pair of short *antennae,* and about what it's eating through a pair of sense organs on its mouth called *palpi.* It has strong jaws called *mandibles* that can chomp through the toughest plants. (But caterpillars never bite people.)

All caterpillars spin silk. This strong fiber is their lifeline, their trail marker, and their building material. A caterpillar has two large glands that make a liquid protein that oozes in two strands from a single opening called the *spinneret* in the caterpillar's lower lip. At the same time, a gummy substance called *sericin* oozes from a second pair of glands. The sericin cements the two strands of silk together as they harden. Adult moths and butterflies can't make silk, but, then, they don't need it.

On the next three segments of the caterpillar's body are three pairs of legs with claws. They will become the legs of the adult moth or butterfly. Most caterpillars also have extra pairs of broad, flat, stumpy legs, called *prolegs,* on their rear segments. Tiny hooks on the bottom of the prolegs give a caterpillar a strong grip.

Along the sides of a caterpillar you can see a line of its breathing holes, called *spiracles.*

Like all insects, caterpillars have an *exoskeleton* instead of an inside skeleton. It is a waterproof skin made of the same tough material that makes up horns, hooves, and fingernails. It's easy for caterpillars to stretch and contract because they have elastic joints between each segment. They can twist and turn better than any human acrobat because they have four thousand muscles. Humans have only 670 skeletal muscles.

A caterpillar's only job is to eat and grow. When its exoskeleton gets too tight, it *molts.* The old skin splits and drops off, leaving a new one underneath. Many caterpillars stick to one kind of food, and even if they are starving, they won't eat anything else. The caterpillar of the monarch butterfly eats nothing but milkweed. Domesticated silkworms eat mulberry leaves. Other kinds of caterpillars aren't so particular. They eat lots of different plants, and one kind of caterpillar eats meat!

Some caterpillars protect themselves by hiding. Their colors and patterns blend in to the background. Others look scary, with big eyespots and long horns. Still others are poisonous or have prickly hairs or spines that birds don't like to eat. Some even make noises that can scare a bird away.

A caterpillar is only one step in the life of a moth or butterfly. There are four stages in all: the egg, the *larva* (which is another name for the caterpillar), the *pupa,* and the adult. The complete change from egg to adult is called a *metamorphosis.*

After a caterpillar has molted four or five times, it makes a *cocoon* if it's a moth, or a *chrysalis* if it's a butterfly, and there it changes into a pupa. The pupa doesn't move, drink, or eat, although it still breathes through its spiracles. During this resting stage, the pupa makes the amazing change from a creepy, crawling creature into a butterfly or moth that can fly away.

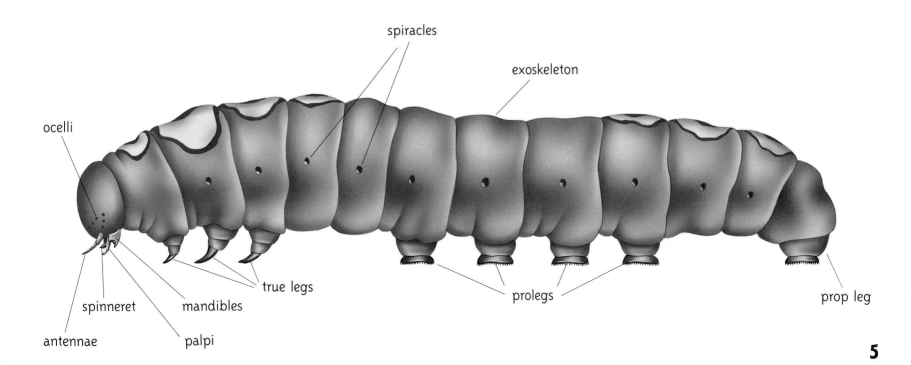

Banded Woolly Bear

If you touch this furry caterpillar, it will curl up like a little hedgehog. The prickly hairs can give you an itchy rash, so it's best to pick up a woolly bear on a stick. Most birds don't like to eat such hairy caterpillars, but skunks don't mind. A hungry skunk will roll a woolly bear around on the ground until the caterpillar's hair falls off.

We see woolly bears most often in the fall as they race across a road, going four feet a minute. That's speedy for a caterpillar! Some people believe they can tell what kind of winter it will be just by looking at the width of the rusty-brown band on a woolly bear. If the caterpillar has a wide band of brown, a late, mild winter is predicted. But if the band is narrow, cold and stormy weather is expected early.

A woolly bear's markings can't really be used to predict the weather. A narrow brown band is only the sign of a young caterpillar. A newly hatched woolly bear is mostly black. Its brown band gets wider as it grows. A woolly bear that hatched in early spring has a wide brown band by late summer. But one that hatched several months later will still have a narrow band in fall. Most caterpillars winter over in a cocoon or chrysalis, but woolly bears hibernate, as real bears do. When winter arrives early, the older woolly bears have already found a safe place to sleep, while the young ones are still scurrying for shelter.

When spring comes, the woolly bears wake up and feast on leaves before they spin cocoons of silk mixed with strands of their long hair. After a few weeks, an Isabella tiger moth comes out of each cocoon. The female moths mate and lay eggs for a new batch of woolly bears to scurry across roads and make us wonder about winter.

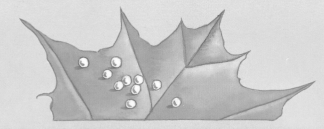

EGGS

ROLLED-UP CATERPILLAR

COCOON

MOTH

7

Tent Caterpillar

Tent caterpillars stick together. Some people call them web worms because they make weblike white tents in apple and cherry trees. In late summer, the female tent caterpillar moth lays a mass of two or three hundred eggs on a tree. She covers them with a waterproof liquid that dries like a coat of hard, shiny varnish to protect them through all kinds of weather. On a sunny spring day, the eggs hatch, and out crawl hundreds of hungry caterpillars. But before they eat, they build a tent where two or three tree branches come together. With hundreds of caterpillars spinning, it doesn't take them long to lay down several layers of tough silk, with space between each layer. The spaces are the wastebins where they can dump their droppings and shed skins, so the rest of the nest stays clean.

If you watched one of these nests all day, you'd see the caterpillars leave three times to look for food—in the early morning, at noon, and just after sundown. Each caterpillar leaves a trail of silk that it will follow home again. The paths paved thickest with silk are those leading to and from the best leaves. Tent caterpillars eat so steadily that they can strip a tree of all its leaves in a day or two.

As they grow, tent caterpillars change their skin five times. After the last molt, late in June, each caterpillar drops to the ground on a strand of silk. Some of them leap off like tiny bungee jumpers. Their last job is to spin their yellow silk cocoons, where the pupa will change into a tiny brown moth that doesn't even have a name of its own. The tent caterpillar moth has no mouth parts. It never eats. It lives only long enough to mate and lay eggs that will hatch into more tent caterpillars.

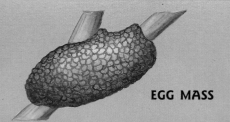

EGG MASS

CATERPILLAR (ACTUAL SIZE)

COCOON

MOTH

9

Cecropia Moth Caterpillar

Nature centers are used to hearing from at least one excited caller each spring who says, "I've found an ugly green monster with red, blue, and yellow bumps. Is it poisonous?" The "monster" turns out to be the caterpillar of the cecropia moth. Even though the fat, five-inch caterpillar looks fearsome, it is neither poisonous nor dangerous.

The cecropia belongs to the family of silk moths. With a wingspan of five or six inches, the cecropia is the biggest moth in North America. We don't see these moths often because they fly at night, and they don't come near houses because they aren't attracted to lights. We don't often see the caterpillars either, because their green color keeps them well hidden among leaves they eat in maple, birch, willow, cherry, or apple trees.

The cecropia's big brown cocoon is hard to see until winter, when the trees are bare. Then you can find one on a low branch, but don't look for a cocoon dangling on a strand of silk. The cecropia takes no chances. The thick cocoon it spins from many layers of silk is fastened lengthwise on a twig, where it will stay put through winter storms.

In order to get out of its tough cocoon in spring, the cecropia moth secretes a liquid that dissolves the silk. When the moth crawls out of the cocoon, it has finished its metamorphosis, and the whole process starts over again. The female lays small clusters of eggs on many different leaves. In ten or twelve days the eggs hatch, and the young caterpillars begin their job of eating—and growing to monster size.

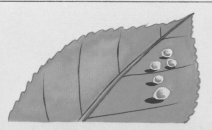

EGGS ON LEAF

COCOON

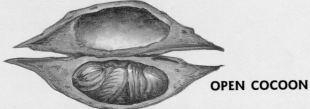

OPEN COCOON

PUPA

MOTH

11

12

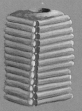

WOODPILE BAG

EVERGREEN BAG

PINECONE BAG

Bagworm

Bagworms carry their houses with them. Each of the eight hundred different kinds of bagworms has its own style of bag built from silk and bits of plants. The adult female bagworm moth doesn't look much like a moth. She has no wings and no legs. Some types have no eyes, antennae, or mouth. She has only one job, and that is to lay her eggs inside her bag. Then she dies. The eggs stay safely inside the mother's bag all winter. When they hatch in spring, the tiny caterpillars eat the leftovers of their eggs before they crawl out to start a life of their own.

A baby bagworm's first chore is to make its own silk sleeping bag, leaving it open at the top so its head can stick out. The bottom is also left open so waste and shed skins can drop out. Then the decorating begins.

One kind of bagworm glues tiny sticks on its silken bag until it looks like a woodpile. An African bagworm arranges small sticks into four walls like a log cabin. Abbott's bagworm builds a small stick bag shaped like a pinecone. The evergreen bagworm's house is covered with needles from cedar or pine trees. In winter you can find the evergreen bagworm's house dangling from the branch of an evergreen tree like a tiny Christmas ornament. Bagworms make their bags bigger as they grow, and they drag their bags with them wherever they go.

When the bagworm caterpillar has molted for the fifth and last time, it fastens its bag to a branch with a silk thread. It will be in this pupa stage for two weeks before it becomes an adult bagworm moth.

LOG CABIN BAG

SILK BAG

MALE MOTH

Lily-Leaf Caterpillar

The word *caterpillar* comes from the Old North French word *catepelose,* which means "hairy cat." It's a strange name, because most cats and caterpillars have only one thing in common: they don't like to swim. But that's not true of the lily-leaf caterpillar, which is a real water baby.

The lily-leaf caterpillar's mother, the china marks moth, lays her eggs on the leaves of plants that grow in ponds and along streambanks. When a caterpillar hatches from one of these eggs, it jumps into the water and heads for a lily pad. There it cuts an oval-shaped chunk from a water lily leaf and fastens it with silk to the underside of another leaf. The caterpillar is sandwiched in the middle of the two leaves, with an opening at one end for its head. The edge of this opening, made of silk, stays snug around the caterpillar's body whenever it pokes out its head to eat leaves. Inside its waterproof sleeping bag, the caterpillar stays dry.

All plants, even those under water, give off oxygen when they make their food. Tucked in its envelope of leaves, the lily-leaf caterpillar takes in oxygen through the spiracles in its body, so that even when its head is in the water, it can still breathe. Hairs on the caterpillar's body keep oxygen in and water out of the sack.

In late fall, when the water gets cold and the plants wither, the lily-leaf caterpillar drops to the bottom of the pond. It hibernates there until spring. When it's ready to change into a pupa, the caterpillar crawls up the stem of a tall water plant and builds a cocoon. A few weeks later, there's a new china marks moth.

WATER LILY LEAVES

CATERPILLAR

CATERPILLAR BETWEEN
TWO LEAVES

MOTH

Green Grappler

Dr. Steven Montgomery is an *entomologist,* a scientist who studies insects. One day when he was looking for insects in the crater of an old volcano in Hawaii, he saw a tiny green inchworm eat a fly. He could hardly believe it. He knew that caterpillars eat plants. But this one was a *carnivore,* a meat eater. Dr. Montgomery called his amazing discovery the green grappler.

An inchworm has no legs in its middle sections. It's also called a looper, or a measuring worm, because of the way it stretches out and pulls its hind legs forward, folding its body up in a loop as it inches along. There are thousands of different kinds of inchworms, all with the scientific name *Geometer,* which means earth measurer.

The green grappler looks like a twig as it holds on to a branch with its hind legs, but instead of munching on leaves like most other inchworms, it waits for live food. When an insect or spider touches the bristles on this caterpillar's back, the grappler swings around faster than the blink of an eye. With the long claws on its six front legs, it grabs the struggling insect, then eats it. These killer caterpillars eat only live insects, and often their prey is heavier than they are.

After this inchworm has molted for the third time, it spins a lacy cocoon. Three weeks later a small, fluttery brown *Eupithecia* (you-pith-uh-SEE-uh) moth emerges and begins to sip nectar from flowers and juices from rotting fruit. The female moth lays about a hundred eggs, which hatch in fourteen days into another batch of carnivorous inchworms hungry for a live, meaty meal.

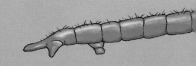

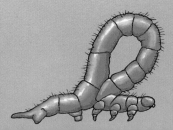

**GREEN GRAPPLER
IN MOTION**

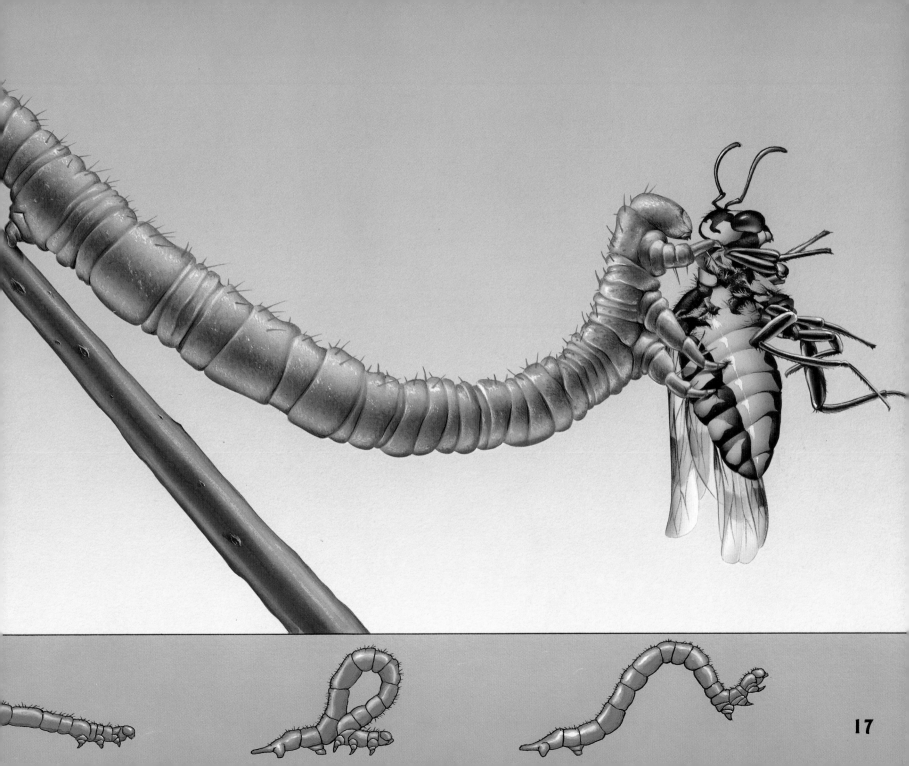

SWEET GUM LEAF

BLACK WALNUT
LEAF

18

Hickory Horned Devil

This caterpillar's name is as wild as its face. The hickory horned devil is the caterpillar of the royal walnut moth, which lives in the eastern United States. When it nibbles its way out of its egg, it is a black caterpillar only a quarter of an inch long. With several spiky horns, it looks like a miniature Chinese dragon. All summer it eats and eats and eats walnut, hickory, pecan, sweet gum, or sumac leaves. As it grows, it molts. The first time its skin splits, it crawls out as a brown caterpillar. On its next molt it changes to tan. After two months, the hickory horned devil is a fat green caterpillar seven inches long.

In fall, the hickory horned devil stops eating. It is ready to become a pupa, but it doesn't spin a silk cocoon like most other moths. Instead, it burrows five or six inches into the ground, and it stays so still you might think it was dead. It begins to shrink. By the time it is only an inch or two long, its exoskeleton splits open and it squirms out for the last time. It is a pupa, in its third stage of life. This shiny brown pupa looks more like a big seed than an animal as it lies buried underground all winter. Sometimes it stays buried for two winters.

But one spring day when the sun has warmed the soil, the pupa splits open and the adult moth crawls out. Its wings dry, and the beautiful orange-and-brown moth flies away. The hickory horned devil has become a royal walnut moth.

PUPA

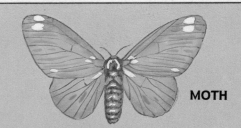

MOTH

Processionary Caterpillar

A procession is a parade, and that's just what these caterpillars seem to love—a parade. Head to tail, like circus elephants, they play follow-the-leader wherever they go. The first caterpillar to leave the nest spins a trail of silk. The second caterpillar spins its thread on top of the first, and each caterpillar in line adds to this pathway paved in silk. Like all caterpillars, they don't see very well, but they keep track of one another by touch.

A French scientist, Jean-Henri Fabre, watched processionary caterpillars as they marched out to look for food and marched back to their nest. He wondered how long they would follow one another. He put the fuzzy caterpillars on the rim of a large tub until there was an unbroken line of them. The caterpillars walked head to tail for 335 laps around the tub rim, until one tired caterpillar finally slipped off and the others followed.

Processionary caterpillars live in Europe, but they are a lot like the tent caterpillars in North America. The adult moth is small, drab, and harmless. The caterpillars are the pests. One kind marches out at night to eat oak leaves, and another eats the needles of pine trees.

Processionaries are pests in another way, too. They are covered with prickly hairs that break off at a touch and leave a person's skin with an itchy, irritating rash. Cattle have been badly injured by these prickly hairs when they wandered into an area where thousands of processionary caterpillars were feeding.

PINE NEEDLES

OAK LEAVES

COCOON

MOTH

21

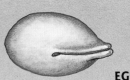

EGG

PUPA

Puss Moth Caterpillar

It's not easy for a caterpillar to fight off a big bird or lizard, but the puss moth caterpillar certainly tries.

The plain brown-and-tan adult puss moth is almost invisible against the bark of a tree trunk, but as a caterpillar, it is anything but plain. When it hatches from its egg, it is a tiny black caterpillar with two long "tails" that some say look like the whiskers of a cat. That's why it's called a puss moth. But as a full-grown, two-inch caterpillar, the puss moth is bright green with a purple saddle on its back. Its red-and-yellow-rimmed face would make a great pattern for a Halloween mask. In place of the last pair of prolegs, this caterpillar has two long rods tipped in red. When it is threatened, it rears up on its hind legs and lashes this weird tail around. At the same time it pulls back its head and puffs up two tiny earlike bumps. If that doesn't scare away the enemy, the caterpillar sprays a stinging fluid called formic acid at the attacker's eyes. Some think that a puss moth gets its name because it spits like a cat, but it doesn't. The spray comes from a gland in the first segment just behind its head.

Puss moths live in Europe and Asia, where they feed on willow and poplar trees. They mix chips of wood from these trees with their own silk to build a cocoon as strong as a walnut shell. In spring, when the adult moth breaks through its pupal case inside the cocoon, sharp bits of that case stay hooked to the moth's head to help the new moth cut through the tough cocoon.

COCOON

MOTH

24

EGG ON LEAF

EARLY LARVA

**PROTRUDING
FORKED GLAND**

Swallowtail Caterpillar

The caterpillar of the swallowtail butterfly has a weird way of protecting itself. When it hatches from an egg, this lumpy brown-and-white caterpillar looks like a bird dropping, and not even the hungriest animal wants to eat that. Then, as it grows and molts, it turns into a colorful caterpillar with a pair of spots on its head that look like bright eyes. These fake eyes will often scare away a predator, but if that isn't enough, swallowtail butterflies have another way of defending themselves.

Each one has a bright red or orange fleshy, forked gland behind its head section. Usually this gland is kept hidden in a pouch, but when the caterpillar is disturbed, the forked gland pokes out and gives off an awful smell. Scientists say that the odor may help keep away parasitic wasps that lay their eggs right on a live caterpillar. When these eggs hatch, the wasp larvae eat the caterpillar. It's the wasp's way of making sure there's a steady supply of fresh meat for its offspring. With enemies like this, it's no wonder caterpillars need several kinds of protection.

Swallowtails were given that name because most of them have tails on their hind wings like the graceful tails of a bird called a swallow. The yellow-and-black-striped tiger swallowtail is the one we see most often flitting around gardens in North America, but the biggest butterfly in the world is also a member of this family. The wings of the Queen Alexandra's birdwing butterfly measure ten or eleven inches from tip to tip.

PREPARING CHRYSALIS

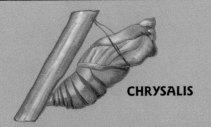
CHRYSALIS

BUTTERFLY

EGG

SHEDDING SKIN

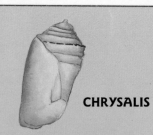

CHRYSALIS

Monarch Caterpillar

To find one of these beautiful striped caterpillars, look on a milkweed plant. Monarchs and milkweed go together. Monarchs are famous for two things—their taste and their travels.

Once a bird has tasted a monarch butterfly or caterpillar, it will not eat another. Monarchs taste awful because the caterpillars eat milkweed. The plant's milky sap contains a mild poison that stays in the caterpillar's body but doesn't hurt it. The poison has a bitter flavor, which the caterpillar doesn't mind but which makes the caterpillar taste disgusting to its predator. That same flavor is passed on when the caterpillar changes into a butterfly.

Monarch butterflies migrate. Late in summer, thousands of delicate butterflies head south. They fly over mountain ranges and long stretches of open ocean to Mexico, Florida, and southern California to spend the winter on the same trees where monarchs have been gathering for centuries. Most of the monarchs that come back north in spring are not the same ones that took the long trip south. On the way north, the females stop to lay their eggs wherever they find milkweed. The caterpillars hatch in four or five days. For the next ten days they eat milkweed, grow, eat some more, and grow some more, until they have molted four times.

The caterpillar then fastens a button of silk to a twig. It hooks its legs into the silk button and hangs upside down. It shivers and shrinks. Its skin splits down the back and falls away. Underneath is a pupa, encased in a chrysalis like a pale green jewel. When the butterfly comes out of the chrysalis twelve days later, it continues the trip north. How does it know where to go if it has never been there? That's still a mystery.

TRANSPARENT CHRYSALIS

BUTTERFLY EMERGING

BUTTERFLY

Tomato Hornworm

If you pick tomatoes in your garden, don't be surprised to find among the leaves a fat green caterpillar with a sword on its tail end. It will probably rear up and pull back its head to show you its big "eyes." The eyespots are fake, but they are often startling enough to scare off a bird that's about to grab the caterpillar for a meal. This is the tomato hornworm, the larva of the tomato hawkmoth. Sometimes they are called sphinx moths.

Hawkmoths are streamlined and speedy. When they fly, their narrow wings beat so fast that you can hear them hum. That's one reason it's easy to mistake them for hummingbirds. Like hummingbirds, they also have long, hollow tongues that fit deep into flowers to reach the sweet nectar. But most hawkmoths fly at sundown, when hummingbirds are asleep. There are a thousand or more different kinds of hawkmoths. The big death's-head hawkmoth of Africa has the pattern of a skull on its back. It squeaks if it's caught, and the huge orange death's-head caterpillar makes a clicking sound if you touch it.

The North American tomato hornworm doesn't make a sound, but it does build a beautiful jug. After its last molt, the hornworm burrows underground to become a pupa. It wiggles and shrinks and turns into a hard, shiny brown jug with a long handle. The jug-handle part holds the long, hollow tongue that the new moth will use to drink nectar from flowers.

EGGS

EGG ON TOMATO LEAF

PUPA

MOTH

30

WHITE OAK

PAWPAW

Saddleback Caterpillar

If you're ever picking pawpaws, keep an eye out for this wild-looking caterpillar that may be feeding on that banana-like fruit. You might also see it on an apple, cherry, or oak tree, or in a cornfield or rose bed. It's hard to tell if a saddleback caterpillar is coming or going, because it can pull its small head back into its body the way a turtle does. And both ends look very much alike, with matched pairs of poisonous horns. Saddlebacks have no legs. Instead they move on paired ridges that work like suction cups, allowing the caterpillar to keep a tight hold on branches and leaves.

Some people call this a nettle caterpillar because its stiff hairs remind them of a prickly nettle plant. Whatever you call it, don't pick it up! Just brushing against its poisonous horns and bristly hairs can give you a painful sting. Its poison and its markings protect it from being eaten. One taste is enough to teach birds to avoid this purplish-brown caterpillar with the brown saddle smack in the center of its bright green back.

There are almost one thousand species of sluglike caterpillars. Most of them live in tropical countries. Of the forty species in North America, the saddleback is the one people remember because it is so colorful. But its parents aren't. The small saddleback caterpillar moth goes almost unnoticed, because it flies at night, and its dull brown wings blend into tree bark, where the female lays her eggs.

After the caterpillar has eaten all summer, it spins a hard-shelled, round cocoon of dark brown silk, where the pupa spends the winter. In spring, the moth pushes aside a lid that was built in to the cocoon and crawls out to start a new batch of saddleback caterpillars.

BLACK CHERRY

MOTH

Glossary

Antennae   movable feelers on an insect's head that also smell and taste

Carnivore   an animal that eats other animals

Caterpillar   the larva of a butterfly or moth

Chrysalis   the hard-shelled case in which a pupa changes to a butterfly

Cocoon   the case a caterpillar spins from silk and sometimes bits of leaves, in which it changes from a pupa into a moth

Entomologist   a scientist who studies insects

Exoskeleton   the hard outer shell or skin of an insect

Larva   the wingless form in which many insects hatch from the egg

Mandibles   an insect's jaws

Metamorphosis   the change an insect's body makes from egg, to larva, to pupa, and finally to adult

Molt   to shed; insects shed their outer skeletons

Ocelli   the twelve tiny eyes on a caterpillar's head

Palpi   a pair of sense organs in the mouth of a caterpillar

Prolegs   flat, stumpy extra "legs" on a caterpillar's rear section

Pupa   the resting stage of an insect just before it changes into an adult

Sericin   the gummy substance that cements the two strands of silk together as they spin out of the caterpillar's spinneret

Spinneret   the opening in a caterpillar's lower lip for spinning silk

Spiracles   the breathing holes in an insect's exoskeleton